11:04 AM

D1604542

Pete & Pillar
the big rain

jeffery stoddard

A story of friendship based on John 15:13

Dedication:
To Keli, my life-giving partner and best friend.

Illustrator: Jeffery Stoddard
Creative Director: Curtis D. Corzine   Editor: Karen Rhodes

Warner Press Kids
educate • nurture • inspire

Published by Warner Press Inc
Text ©2007 by Jefferey Stoddard
Illustrations ©2007 by Warner Press Inc
All rights reserved
ISBN: 1-59317-203-6
Printed in Singapore

High in the Shady Mountains, where the Crystal River tumbled over big boulders and gently flowed through a lush, green valley, there was a town where two unusual friends lived, Pete and Pillar.

Pete, a mighty diesel truck with his huge wheels and a tall,
bright smokestack, was a hauler. Pete hauled gravel, dirt and giant rocks.
He carried gigantic yellow digging machines
to construction sites high up rocky roads.
He even hauled long beams
for building bridges.

Pillar was a bulldozer. He rumbled along on heavy steel tracks, pushing rocks and piling tall mounds of dirt with his thick steel blade. He cleared the way for new roads. He leveled hillsides for new barns. He even dug streambeds out for new ponds.

Pete and Pillar were best friends...which may seem odd, because everybody knows haulers don't talk to diggers.

But Pete and Pillar didn't listen to what others said.

They were friends. Not just friends...

they were best friends.

Every day their friendship grew stronger as they worked side by side.

In the winter when the snow drifts on the pass were so deep

even the road plows stayed in the shed,

Pillar cleared the way and

Pete spread the sand.

When

Pete's huge wheels dug into soft sand and wouldn't go, Pillar came to the rescue.

They were such good friends that one day they scraped into each other on purpose. Pete left a splotch of red paint on Pillar and Pillar left a yellow splotch on Pete.

9

Pillar's battery died.

Pete had power to share....

Sometimes during the night, while all the others were sleeping, Pete and Pillar would have a belching contest.

Pillar usually won.

One day Jake, an old dump truck came to Pete in the yard.

"Listen Petey, you should stay away from those diggers," said Jake. "They smell like dusty grease and old engine oil. They can't move fast like a hauler. Yup," said the old truck, "most of them have broken windows, worn rubber tires and rusty tracks. They're rusty, smelly, slow grumps, they are." "You watch out Pete," said Jake. "Bulldozers can't be trusted."

"And if you know what's best for you, you'll stay away from 'em."

That same day a long road grader named John stopped Pillar. "Pillar, we need to talk," said John. "Stay away from haulers. They're not like us. They can't dig or push, pile or lift. All they can do is haul. They complain if the load is too heavy or too wide, especially if they have to drive in the mud."

John looked both ways and then whispered, "They hate mud. All they want to do is move fast on smooth roads, dump their load and move on. That hauler may say he's your friend today, but wait until you really need him. You'll turn around and he'll be long gone."

Neither Pete nor Pillar listened to the rest of the machines.

They were inseparable,

faithful,

best,

best

friends.

And then it began to rain.

The Sky

grew black and deep rumbles of thunder echoed across the valley. High on the mountain peaks the rain came splashing and tumbling down the steep slopes.

D<small>rops</small> turned into trickles that turned into streams that became a raging flood. Down the valley the brown water plunged, uprooting trees and washing out bridges. The water rushed over the dam and toward the town.

All the machines hurried back to their sheds to get out of the rain. If there is one thing all machines fear it's rain. Rainwater creeps into joints and axles, pieces and parts. And then smooth, shiny metal parts become rusty and stiff. And when parts become rusty and stiff, they stop working. That's when machines are parked behind the shed…

forever.

Machines don't like rain.

19

Pete and Pillar watched as the rushing water rose higher and higher, eating away at the riverbank that protected the town.

Pillar knew what he had to do. If the bank caved in, the town would be flooded. With his big, strong tracks and huge blade, he knew he had to push more rocks onto the bank. He crawled into the raging, brown water. The rushing flood swirled around his mighty engine, steam billowed out as the cold water washed against him. Pillar dug deep into the riverbed and pushed a huge boulder up to the bank. But the water continued to rise. He glanced up to see Pete with panic in his headlights.

Pillar's engine sputtered and coughed as
he tried to push another huge boulder to the bank.
He glanced up to make sure Pete was okay.

Pete was gone.
Just like the other digger had said,
"When you really need him, he'll be gone."
Pillar's heart sank.

Then suddenly, the water stopped rising.

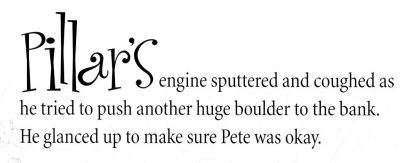

22

Exhausted and sad, Pillar slowly climbed out of the river. How could his friend leave him just when Pillar needed him most? Caked in thick mud and dripping with dirty water he looked down and saw the muddy tracks his friend had left. Pillar decided to find Pete and ask him why he disappeared right when Pillar needed him the most.

As the rain stopped, Pillar followed his friend's muddy tracks up the mountain above the town. Little streams of water ran down the road in the deep ruts left by Pete. In one place Pillar could see where his wheels spun, slipped and nearly slid off the edge.

24

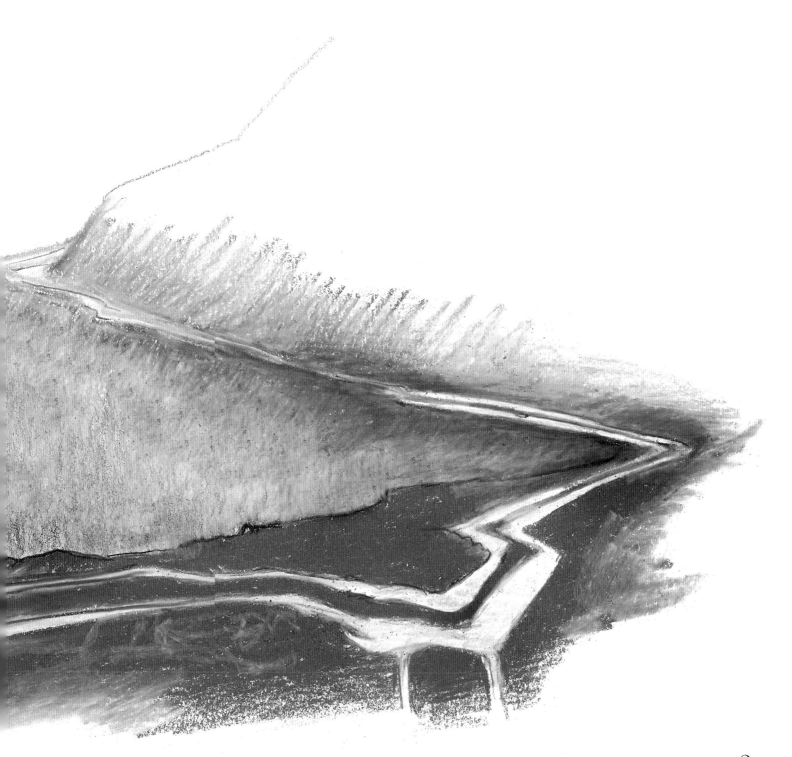

Pillar followed the soggy ruts onto the dam high above the town and there—he could hardly believe his eyes. He saw the tip of a bright smokestack sticking out from where the dam had nearly burst. Pete had driven up the muddy, narrow road to the dam and plugged the hole…

with himself.

Pete had sacrificed himself to save his best friend

and the town.

Pillar rushed back to town as fast as his tracks would roll. He called all the machines—haulers and diggers—to come help him. It took all of them working together in a long line to pull, dig and push the mighty truck from the muck. Pete was covered in gooey mud from his hood ornament to his taillights.

There was so much mud his wheels refused to roll.

So they carried him.

Together the haulers and diggers scraped and
scooped and sprayed and wiped away mounds of mucky, sticky
mud off Pete. Pillar stayed by his side night and day as he
slowly came back to life.

30

Finally all the mud was gone and Pete was like a shiny new truck once again...

All except for that little splotch of yellow on his fender.

And that would never come off.

From that day on, diggers and haulers in that small town worked side by side as friends. And if you listen closely to diggers and haulers working in your town, you can hear them toot their horns to each other.

Yup. They're talking about Pete and Pillar.

Two best friends.